THE BEST OF
CLAY POT
COOKING

THE BEST OF
CLAY POT
COOKING

Dana Jacobi

Food Photography by Elizabeth Watt

CollinsPublishersSanFrancisco
A Division of HarperCollins*Publishers*

First published in USA 1995 by Collins Publishers San Francisco
1160 Battery Street, San Francisco, CA 94111

Produced by Smallwood and Stewart, Inc.,
New York City

© 1995 Smallwood and Stewart, Inc.

Editor: Mary MacVean
Food Styling: Dora Jonassen
Prop Styling: Susan Byrnes

Photography credits: E.R. Degginger/Picture Perfect: p. 26.
Robert V. Eckert Jr./Picture Perfect: p. 36.
Nick Nicholson/Image Bank: p. 43. W.D. Adams/Picture Perfect:
p. 61. Bob Higbee/Picture Perfect: p. 73. Naomi Duguid/Asia
Access: p. 1; 83. Mike S. Yamashita: endpapers

Jacobi, Dana.
The best of clay pot cooking / recipes by Dana Jacobi;
food photography by Elizabeth Watt.
p.   cm.
Includes index.
ISBN 0-00-225051-9
1. Clay pot cookery. I. Title.
TX825.5.J33   1995   95-10823
641.5'89—dc20   CIP

Printed in China

1 3 5 7 9 10 8 6 4 2

Contents

Introduction

Clay pots were among our first cooking vessels. In various shapes and sizes, they have been used in the kitchen since at least Roman times, and are still commonly found from China to Morocco, South America, and beyond. And for good reason. Clay pots offer easy ways to cook an astonishing range of healthy, delicious dishes. Enclosed in clay, foods stay succulent and cook beautifully, often without any added fat, as their flavors mingle, concentrate, and enrich one another.

Many people are amazed at how delectable a chicken is when roasted in clay. But that is just the start. Following are recipes for main dishes, soups, vegetables, breads, even desserts. Many of these recipes simplify cooking to one pot: Just measure the ingredients into the clay pot, place the pot in the oven, then serve. There are meatless main dishes, lean choices that call for no fat at all, as well as lavish dishes for special occasions ~ all exploring the versatility of cooking in clay.

The most common clay pots ~ unglazed red clay cookers that are soaked in water before using, and the glazed, heavy, open casserole-type dish from Spain called a cazuela ~ are amazingly versatile. Use the cooker to roast a turkey without basting. And to produce rich soups or perfectly baked desserts. Try braising rice or baking Peach-Blackberry Crumple in the cazuela. In all these dishes, flavors emerge fresh and clear. Beans cooked in a clay pot come out velvety. Baking in clay also brilliantly preserves the bright, true colors of vegetables.

This book offers recipes for dishes from 15 countries, some adapted to modern tastes or available ingredients and some made in the traditional clay pots, such as the Moroccan tagine. In an age of high-tech equipment, health-consciousness, and the desire for easy, satisfying meals, the pleasures of clay-pot cooking prove the adage, "Everything old is new again."

Dana Jacobi

TYPES OF CLAY POTS

Red Clay Pot: Most of the recipes in this book can be made with an unglazed red clay pot. This porous, lidded pot is the most versatile of all clay cookers. Before going into the oven, soak red clay pots in water. The moisture absorbed by the pot will be released during baking, keeping food moist and making this cooker ideal for many soups as well as braised meats. This pot comes in various sizes of which the three- and four-quart sizes are most useful. Romertopf is the most common brand.

Other pots used in the book include:
Boston Bean Pot: This squat-bodied, narrow-mouthed glazed pot is usually dark brown inside and halfway down the outside. It may or may not be covered. The pot's curved, thick sides ensure slow, even cooking ~ traditionally the pot would have been buried in hot coals. The 2½-quart size is the most versatile.
Bread Baker: This large, unglazed pot has a high, domed top. It acts like a brick oven within the oven, browning bread evenly and producing an extra-crisp crust. It comes in round and long shapes. La Cloche is the most common brand.

Cazuela: This shallow, open, round dish comes from Spain. Glazed inside, it is good for some kinds of braising and for casseroles ~ its thick walls distribute heat gently and evenly during oven cooking. *Cazuelas* come in several sizes and are pretty enough for the table.

Fish Baker: A shallow oval dish, sometimes in the shape of a fish, with a glazed bottom and an unglazed top. Only the top needs to be soaked; this keeps the fish moist. The glazed bottom prevents the fish from sticking.

Tagine: This round North African pot with a shallow bottom and conical top is traditionally used over a charcoal brazier but works perfectly set on a flame-tamer on a gas or electric stove. The pots come glazed and unglazed. Sizes for six or eight people are most useful. (*Tagine* is also the name of a stew made in this cooker.)

Tian: This rectangular, glazed dish made in Provence resembles a shallow terrine and is used for making *tians*, or gratins. It is difficult to find in the United States; a cazuela or rectangular ovenproof dish can be substituted.

Sand Pot: The Chinese make this covered pot from a mixture of clay and sand. It is glazed inside and comes in several shapes and sizes. Use this pot on the stove, set on a flame-tamer, for moist stews and chunky soups.

CARING FOR CLAY POTS

Clay pots are surprisingly durable. Porous clay pots, made from a blend of clays and fired at more than 1700°F, can last for years if treated properly.

Curing:
Scrub a new clay pot well with dishwashing liquid and hot water. Unglazed pots, such as the Romertopf, need no curing, but avoid recipes with fish or pronounced flavors for the first use. Roasting a chicken, with its gentler flavors, is a good way to start one off.

Tagines should be cured by filling the bottom with water, and adding a halved onion, a carrot cut into pieces, a bay leaf, and a tablespoon of olive oil. Cover and cook for an hour, then let the liquid cool in the pot.

Fill a new sand pot or cazuela with water and simmer it for an hour, then let cool before emptying.

Six rules for cooking in clay:
1. Always soak unglazed pots such as the Romertopf in water before using. To soak, place both the top and bottom in the sink and fill with enough lukewarm water to cover both pieces. If you are using a

large pot, it's fine to nest the bottom inside the top. Soak a new unglazed clay pot for 30 minutes the first time you use it; after that, soak it for 15 minutes every time you use it and drain it thoroughly.

2. Never subject a clay pot to quick or extreme changes in temperature. Don't add cold liquid to a hot pot or pour boiling liquid into an empty cold one, or the pot may crack. Always place a hot clay pot and its cover on potholders. Wait until the pot cools before placing it in the sink for washing. Some clay pots must be placed in a cold oven. Others should be used on a flame-tamer on the stove. The recipes in this book indicate which procedure to follow.

3. When opening a pot after cooking, tilt the cover away from you to prevent the steam from hitting your face.

4. Use long ovenproof mitts when handling a hot clay pot.

5. Do not store cooked food in a clay pot; the flavors will seep into the clay and will be hard to remove.

6. Never use scouring powder or steel wool on a clay pot. Scrub pots with a fiber or nylon pad. For extra cleaning, fill the pot with hot water, baking soda, and dishwashing liquid, then let it soak overnight. If burnt food still clings to the pot, refill it with water, add baking soda, and place it in an oven. Set the temperature to 400°F, cook for an hour, then let the pot cool and wash again.

Butternut Squash Soup
with Chestnut "Croutons"

*A dash of orange juice and pieces of velvety chestnut add vibrant
contrasts to the sweet, autumn flavors and bright, clear color brought out by
cooking this soup in clay. This easy method also uses no fat at all.*

1 small butternut squash,
   halved, seeded & cut into
   1-inch pieces
1 medium onion, chopped
1 large Cortland or Rome
   Beauty apple, peeled,
   cored & diced

4 cups chicken broth
2 sprigs fresh thyme
1 bay leaf
¼ teaspoon salt
¼ teaspoon black pepper
½ pound chestnuts
⅓ cup orange juice

In a soaked 3-quart clay pot, combine the squash, onion, apple, and 1 cup of the broth. Cover the pot and place it in a cold oven. Set the oven temperature to 450°F and cook for 30 minutes, or until the mixture is soft.

Add the remaining broth, the thyme, bay leaf, and the salt and pepper. Cover and cook for 30 minutes more.

Meanwhile, with a small sharp knife, cut an X in the rounded side of each chestnut, being sure to pierce the papery inner covering. Cook the chestnuts in a large pot of boiling water for about 20 minutes, until soft. Cool the chestnuts just enough to be able to handle them. Peel them and break each one into 3 or 4 pieces.

Remove the thyme and the bay leaf from the soup. Purée the soup in a blender. (Using a food processor won't give as smooth a result.) Stir in the orange juice and adjust the seasoning if necessary. Serve garnished with the chestnuts. **Serves 6.**

Green Split Pea Soup

*Cooking this thick meatless soup in a clay pot eliminates the
likelihood of scorching, because the pot stays moist.
If you wish, add a few slices of kielbasa or minced ham to give
a smoky flavor to this otherwise fat-free dish.*

1 pound green split peas,
   picked over & rinsed

2 carrots, cut into 1-inch pieces

1 leek (white part only),
   cut lengthwise in half

1 medium onion, halved
   lengthwise

4 large garlic cloves, peeled

1 sprig fresh thyme, or
   ½ teaspoon dried

½ teaspoon finely chopped
   fresh rosemary, or
   ¼ teaspoon crushed dried

1 bay leaf

¼ teaspoon ground cardamom

Salt & black pepper

Fresh minced dill, for garnish
   (optional)

Place the peas in a soaked 4-quart clay pot. Add the carrots, leek, onion, garlic, thyme, rosemary, bay leaf, and cardamom. Pour in 6 cups of water. Cover the pot and place it in a cold oven. Set the oven temperature to 450°F and cook for 1 hour to 1 hour and 15 minutes, until the peas are soft. Check the soup by stirring: the peas should be soft and mushy.

With a slotted spoon, remove the carrots, leek, onion, and the thyme sprig, if used. Mash the soft garlic cloves into the soup. Season to taste with the salt and pepper. Serve garnished with the dill, if desired. Or add vegetable broth, thinning the soup to a texture you prefer. **Serves 8 to 10.**

Moroccan Stuffed Red Snapper

Morocco has more than 1,000 miles of coast so local markets are filled with beautifully displayed fresh fish and seafood. Serve this intriguingly spiced dish with couscous made with chicken broth and garnished with toasted sliced almonds.

1 medium onion, halved lengthwise & cut into ½-inch-thick slices

1 medium green bell pepper, seeded & cut lengthwise into ½-inch strips

4 large plum tomatoes, halved, seeded & cut lengthwise into ½-inch slices

2 large shallots, thinly sliced

⅓ cup dried currants

⅓ cup pitted Calamata olives

¼ cup minced fresh cilantro

¼ cup minced fresh flat-leaf parsley

¾ teaspoon cinnamon

½ teaspoon ground cardamom

½ teaspoon ground ginger

Salt & black pepper

Two ¾- to 1-pound red snapper fillets, cleaned & gutted

In a large bowl, toss together the onion, pepper, tomatoes, shallots, currants, olives, cilantro, parsley, cinnamon, cardamom, and ginger until blended. Season with salt and pepper to taste.

Spread one third of the vegetable mixture over the bottom of a soaked 4-quart clay pot. Place one fillet over the vegetables, skin side down, then cover with one third of the vegetable mixture.

Place the remaining fillet, skin side up, on top of the vegetable mixture in the pot. Distribute the remaining vegetable mixture over the fish. Cover the pot and place it in a cold oven. Set the oven temperature to 450°F and cook for about 30 minutes, until the fish is flaky and opaque throughout but still moist.

Serve immediately. **Serves 4 .**

Salmon with Ginger & Lime

Clay cooking keeps fish moist while bringing out its flavor to perfection. The creamy sauce is so intensely flavored that you need only a little of it. Any leftover sauce can be reheated in a microwave oven or in the top of a double boiler; try it on boiled potatoes.

Fish:

1 large lime

1¼ pounds salmon fillet, in 1 piece

1 teaspoon salt

¼ teaspoon black pepper

One 1-inch piece ginger, peeled & finely julienned

Sauce:

1 tablespoon minced shallots

2 teaspoons soy sauce

¼ teaspoon celery seed

½ cup (1 stick) unsalted butter, cut into small pieces & well chilled

4 thin lime wedges, for garnish (optional)

Prepare the fish: Remove the zest from half the lime. Cut the zest into julienne. Cut the lime in half lengthwise. Squeeze the juice from the zested half. Cut the other half lengthwise into 8 thin wedges and set aside.

Place the fish skin side down in a clay fish baker or other covered 3-quart clay pot. If using a clay fish baker, soak only the unglazed top. Season the fish with salt and pepper to taste. Sprinkle the ginger, lime zest, and lime juice evenly over the fish. Arrange the lime wedges in a row along the center of the fish. Cover and place in a cold oven. Set the oven temperature to 425°F and cook for 20 to 25 minutes, until the fish is opaque throughout.

Meanwhile, prepare the sauce: Combine the shallots, soy sauce, celery seed, and ¼ cup of water in a small nonreactive saucepan. Bring to a boil

over medium heat and boil until the liquid is reduced to 1 tablespoon. Reduce the heat to low. Using a wire whisk, vigorously whisk in the butter, one piece at a time. Allow each piece to be incorporated into the sauce before adding more. The sauce will gradually thicken to the consistency of whipping cream.

Remove and discard the ginger, lime zest, and lime wedges from the salmon. Cut the salmon into 4 pieces. Arrange the fish on 4 dinner plates. Spoon 2 tablespoons of the sauce over each serving and top with a wedge of lime, if desired. Pour the remaining sauce into a small bowl or sauceboat and pass separately. **Serves 4.**

Shrimp & Ham Jambalaya

*While not traditional, a generous tot of sherry complements the shrimp
and adds complexity to this Creole favorite. The steaming rice cooks the shrimp rapidly,
so be careful not to let them get overcooked, particularly if they are on the
small side. Leave their tails sticking out of the rice so you can easily test when they are
done. Be sure to pass a bottle of hot sauce for those who want an added kick.*

I cup long-grain rice

4 or 5 chopped canned plum
  tomatoes, plus enough of
  their juice to make I cup

I cup finely chopped onions

¼ cup finely chopped
  green bell pepper

I bay leaf

½ teaspoon dried oregano

¼ teaspoon dried thyme

½ teaspoon salt

½ cup dry sherry

12 to 16 medium shrimp

I cup cubed Black Forest ham
  (about 6 ounces)

Chopped fresh flat-leaf parsley,
  for garnish

In a soaked 3-quart clay pot, combine the rice, tomatoes, onions, bell pepper, bay leaf, oregano, thyme, salt, and sherry. Add 1½ cups of water and stir to blend. Cover the pot and place it in a cold oven. Set the oven temperature to 450°F and cook for 40 minutes (the rice will be al dente).

Meanwhile, peel the shrimp, leaving the tail and the shell up to the first joint.

Stir the ham and shrimp into the rice. Cover the pot and cook for 8 to 10 minutes, just until the shrimp are pink and firm. Remove and discard the bay leaf. Garnish with the parsley. Serve immediately. **Serves 4.**

Mediterranean Fish Stew

French and Spanish influences combine in this golden fish dish. The tarragon is typically French, while saffron and almonds were added to Spanish cooking centuries ago with the arrival of the Arabs from North Africa. Firm-fleshed fish, such as cod or scrod, halibut, or turbot, work best. Unlike most fish dishes, this one improves after it sits, so consider making it in the morning or even a day ahead. Simply leave the fish slightly underdone so it will be perfectly cooked after the stew is reheated. For a satisfying meal, all this needs is crusty bread.

I tablespoon unsalted butter
I medium onion, chopped
I garlic clove, minced
Two 6-ounce bottles clam juice
I cup chicken broth
I cup dry white wine
4 to 5 ripe plum tomatoes,
   seeded & chopped (I cup)

2 teaspoons chopped
   fresh tarragon
Pinch of saffron, crushed
I½ pounds firm white fish
   fillets, cut into 4 pieces
Salt & black pepper
2 tablespoons toasted
   sliced almonds

In a medium-size skillet, melt the butter. Add the onion and garlic and sauté for about 5 minutes, until the onion is soft. Transfer the mixture to a soaked 3-quart clay pot.

Add the clam juice, broth, wine, tomatoes, 1 teaspoon of the tarragon, and the saffron. Cover the pot and place it in a cold oven. Set the oven temperature to 450°F and cook for 20 minutes.

Remove the pot from the oven, add the fish and cover. Return to the oven until the fish cooks through, 5 to 12 minutes, depending on the thickness of the fish. Season with salt and pepper to taste. Ladle the stew and fish into 4 serving bowls. Garnish with the remaining tarragon and the almonds, and serve.

If making the stew ahead, add the fish to the clay pot, stir to coat well, then

transfer the stew to a large plastic container. The fish will partially cook in the stew. Let cool to room temperature, cover, and refrigerate until ready to serve. Transfer the stew to a pot and bring to a simmer on the stove top until heated through. **Serves 4.**

Marmitako

Marmitako is a simple fisherman's dish, from the Basque provinces along the border of northern Spain, made using tuna or bonito. Serve with a crisp white wine, such as Portuguese vinho verde.

3 tablespoons olive oil

½ medium onion, sliced

2 garlic cloves, finely chopped

4 plum tomatoes, seeded & chopped

¼ cup drained capers

4 all-purpose potatoes, peeled & cut into ½-inch slices

2 cups chicken broth

1 pound fresh tuna, cut into 4 pieces

Salt & black pepper

Preheat the oven to 400°F.

In a medium-size skillet, heat 2 tablespoons of the oil over medium-high heat. Add the onion and cook, stirring occasionally, for 3 to 4 minutes, until soft. Add the garlic and tomatoes and cook, stirring occasionally, for about 10 minutes, until the tomatoes are soft. Stir in the capers.

Meanwhile, arrange the potato slices in the bottom of a 12¼-inch cazuela or other shallow heatproof dish, overlapping the slices.

Spread the tomato and onion mixture over the potatoes. Pour over the broth. Place the cazuela in the oven and bake for about 20 minutes, until the potatoes are almost cooked.

Sprinkle the tuna slices lightly with salt and pepper to taste. Place on top of the potatoes and bake for 5 to 8 minutes, until the tuna is opaque throughout. Adjust the seasoning if necessary. Serve hot or at room temperature. **Serves 4.**

Clay-Roasted Turkey

Clay cooking makes roasting a turkey unexpectedly fast and easy. You also get remarkably grease-free stuffing. Simply roast the bird in the covered pot, without greasing its skin or adding any liquid. The moisture in the pot eliminates any need for basting or turning. A small turkey will even brown gloriously in the covered pot. Use a fresh turkey; the meat will be much moister than that of a frozen bird.

One 10- to 12-pound
    fresh turkey
6 cups stuffing of your choice
1 carrot, cut into 1-inch pieces
1 medium onion, coarsely
    chopped

1 stalk celery, cut into
    1-inch pieces
2 to 3 sprigs fresh flat-leaf
    parsley

Remove the giblets and neck. Discard the liver. Rinse the turkey, giblets, and neck, and set the giblets and neck aside. Dry the turkey inside and out with paper towels.

Loosely pack the stuffing into the central and neck cavities of the turkey. Pull the neck flap down and tuck it under the bird.

Truss the turkey and place in a soaked 6½-quart clay pot. Fold the first joint of each wing so it lies against the side of the pot (this may require breaking the ten-dons at the joint). Cover the pot and place it in a cold oven. Set the oven temperature to 350°F and cook the turkey for 2 hours. (Do not open the oven.)

Meanwhile, place the gizzards and neck in a medium-size saucepan. Add the carrot, onion, celery, and parsley. Add 4 cups of cold water and bring just to a boil over medium-high heat. Reduce the heat and simmer, partially covered, for about 2 hours, until the liquid is reduced by two-thirds; skim off any foam that forms on top. Strain out the

Turkey farm

solids and reserve 1 cup of broth.

When the turkey has cooked for 2 hours, check the temperature of the thigh meat at its thickest part with a quick-read thermometer (be sure the thermometer is not touching the bone). The turkey is done when the thigh meat reaches 180°F. If the turkey needs additional browning, uncover and continue cooking for 30 minutes to 1 hour.

Check the temperature of the stuffing. If it has not reached 160°F, remove the turkey to a serving platter and cover with aluminum foil. Scoop the stuffing from the center cavity into a buttered baking dish, and bake, uncovered, until the temperature reaches 160°F to 170°F. (The stuffing in the front should be done at the same time as the turkey.) Let the turkey rest for 20 minutes before carving.

Meanwhile, pour the pan juices into a clear measuring cup and let sit until the fat rises to the top. Remove the fat, and combine with the 1 cup of the hot strained turkey broth. Pour into a sauceboat to pass with the turkey. **Serves 8.**

Clay-Roasted Chicken

This is the most popular clay pot dish, probably because the chicken browns nicely while staying moist. You get rich, natural gravy, and even the cleanup is simple. For variety, slip thin slices of lemon, sprigs of tarragon, slivers of garlic, or a mixture of lavender and thyme under the skin of the chicken before trussing it. The lemon is especially good for keeping the leaner, firmer meat of free-range chickens moist.

One 4- to 4½-pound chicken
1 medium onion, cut
    into 8 wedges
1 stalk celery, cut into 8 pieces
1 large carrot, cut into 8 pieces
1 tablespoon unsalted butter,
    softened
¾ cup chicken broth

Rinse the chicken and dry it with paper towels. Truss the chicken. Place the onion, celery, and carrot in a layer in a soaked 3-quart clay pot. Rub the chicken all over with the butter and place breast side up on the bed of vegetables. Pour the broth over the chicken. Cover the pot and place it in a cold oven. Set the oven temperature to 450°F and cook the chicken for 1 hour and 15 minutes, or until the legs move easily and the skin is lightly browned. Transfer the chicken to a platter. Let stand for 15 to 20 minutes before carving.

Meanwhile, pour the pan juices into a small bowl and let sit until ready to serve. Before serving, skim off any fat that has risen to the top. Carve the chicken and serve with the pan juices. **Serves 6.**

Indonesian Beggar's Chicken

Tamarind, lime, cilantro, and a touch of chile give this chicken its classic Southeast Asian flavor. Indian and Asian food stores carry tamarind paste. Serve the chicken with fragrant basmati or jasmine rice.

1 medium onion, sliced
2 tablespoons chopped
    fresh cilantro
3 garlic cloves, chopped
1 tablespoon tamarind paste
1 *serrano* chile, seeded
    & chopped

1 anchovy fillet, drained
    & chopped
2 tablespoons dark soy sauce
1 tablespoon fresh lime juice
¼ teaspoon salt
½ teaspoon black pepper
One 4½- to 5-pound chicken

In a blender, combine the onion, cilantro, garlic, tamarind paste, chile, anchovy, soy sauce, lime juice, salt, and pepper. Blend to a paste.

Rinse the chicken, dry with paper towels, and place on a plate. Smear the inside of the chicken with one third of the spice paste. Smear the remaining paste over the outside of the chicken. Cover the chicken loosely with plastic wrap and refrigerate for 1 to 2 hours.

Transfer the chicken to a soaked 3-quart clay pot. Cover the pot and place it in a cold oven. Set the oven temperature to 450°F and cook the chicken for 1 hour and 25 minutes, or until the drumsticks wiggle easily.

Remove the chicken to a serving plate. Let stand for 10 to 15 minutes before carving.

Meanwhile, pour the pan juices from the pot into a small bowl and let sit until ready to serve. Just before serving, skim off any fat that has risen to the top. Carve the chicken and serve with the pan juices. **Serves 6.**

Singapore Chicken Curry

*Coconut milk and ground nuts make this gentle curry creamy and rich.
The lemongrass and curry leaves, sold at Indian and Southeast Asian markets,
lend an aromatic note. Pass toasted sliced almonds, mango chutney,
and a mixture of currants and golden raisins to garnish the dish. Serve
with an aromatic rice, such as basmati or jasmine.*

¼ cup roasted cashew nuts

¼ cup macadamia nuts

3 large shallots, chopped

3 garlic cloves, chopped

3 curry leaves (optional)

One 1-inch piece ginger,
  peeled & chopped

1 teaspoon ground turmeric

½ teaspoon cayenne

½ teaspoon ground cumin

½ teaspoon ground fennel seeds

⅛ teaspoon ground cloves

1 teaspoon salt

¼ teaspoon black pepper

One 13½-ounce can
  coconut milk

2 whole boneless & skinless
  chicken breasts, cut into
  1-inch pieces

Three 2-inch pieces lemongrass,
  halved lengthwise

1 bay leaf

In a blender, combine the nuts, shallots, garlic, curry leaves, if desired, the ginger, turmeric, cayenne, cumin, fennel, cloves, salt, and pepper. Add the coconut milk and blend to a paste.

Place the chicken in a soaked 3-quart clay pot. Add the lemongrass and bay leaf. Pour the coconut milk mixture over the chicken and stir to coat well. Cover the pot and place it in a cold oven. Set the oven temperature to 450°F and cook for 40 minutes, or until the chicken is cooked through. Remove the lemongrass and bay leaf. Serve in bowls over rice. **Serves 4.**

Chicken Tagine with Green Olives & Preserved Lemon

*If you can, make this dish as Moroccan women have for centuries,
in the cone-topped clay cooker that gives it its name ~ otherwise a Dutch oven
works well. Traditionally, preserved lemons require curing in salt for
at least two weeks. But this method, discovered by Paula Wolfert, takes only
five days. And, you can preserve just one or two lemons instead of
making a large batch. Try them chopped and mixed with green olives for an
hors d'oeuvre, or place one inside a chicken before roasting,
or chopped, in the cavity of a fish.*

8 large chicken thighs, skinned

¾ cup finely chopped onion

½ cup finely chopped
    fresh cilantro

½ cup finely chopped
    flat-leaf parsley

2 garlic cloves, minced

1 teaspoon ground cumin

1 teaspoon ground ginger

1 teaspoon sweet paprika

½ teaspoon black pepper

¼ teaspoon saffron, crushed

2 cups Greek green olives, such
    as Ionian or Nafplion

½ Moroccan Preserved Lemon,
    chopped (see Note), or
    lemon juice to taste

Juice of 1 lemon

Salt & black pepper

Arrange the chicken thighs in one layer in a medium-size tagine or Dutch oven. Sprinkle the onion, cilantro, parsley, garlic, cumin, ginger, paprika, ½ teaspoon of the pepper, and saffron over the chicken.

Add 2 cups of water and cover the pot.

If using a tagine, set it on a flame-tamer over medium heat. If using a Dutch oven, set over medium-high heat; the flame-tamer is not necessary. Bring to a boil. Immediately reduce the heat and simmer gently for 30 minutes.

Meanwhile, pit the olives: Place the olives, one at a time, on a cutting board and smash firmly with the flat side of a heavy knife. Remove the pit.

Add the olives, preserved lemon, and lemon juice to the tagine and continue cooking about 20 minutes, until the chicken meat is falling off the bones. Season with salt and pepper to taste. **Serves 4.**

NOTE: To prepare the Moroccan Preserved Lemons: Scrub 2 lemons very well to remove any wax or pesticide residues. Using the tip of a sharp paring knife, cut 8 slits in each lemon, starting ½ inch below the top and ending ½ inch above the bottom. Take care to cut only through the zest and white pith part of the skin; do not cut into the flesh.

Place the lemons in a small nonreactive saucepan. Add ½ cup coarse salt and enough water to cover. Bring to a boil and boil gently for about 15 minutes, until the peels are very soft.

Meanwhile, wash a 1-pint glass jar and lid in very hot, soapy water and rinse well.

Place the lemons in the jar. Add enough of the cooking liquid to fill the jar, leaving ½ inch of headspace. Cover and refrigerate for 5 days before using.

The lemons will keep for up to 1 week in the refrigerator after they are cured.

Sesame Chicken

Cooking in a clay pot gives you a particularly succulent version of this popular dish. Serve it hot, right from the pot, accompanied by steamed broccoli and rice. Or let the chicken cool, shred the meat, and serve it as a salad tossed in its velvety, nutty sauce.

½ cup smooth peanut butter

One 1-inch piece ginger, peeled & minced

3 garlic cloves, minced

1 teaspoon Chinese five-spice powder

½ cup chicken broth

1 tablespoon soy sauce

2 tablespoons sake (rice wine) or sherry

1 tablespoon Chinese red rice vinegar or red wine vinegar

1 teaspoon roasted sesame oil

¼ to ½ teaspoon hot-pepper flakes

½ teaspoon black pepper

2 whole chicken breasts, skinned & split

⅓ cup chopped scallions (white & tender green parts), for garnish

In a medium-size bowl, combine the peanut butter, ginger, garlic, five-spice powder, broth, soy sauce, sake, vinegar, sesame oil, hot-pepper flakes, and pepper, mixing until well blended.

Arrange the chicken breasts in one layer in a soaked 3-quart clay pot. Pour the peanut mixture over the chicken, turning to coat well. Cover the pot and place it in a cold oven. Set the oven temperature to 450°F and cook for 45 minutes, or until the chicken is cooked through.

Transfer the chicken to a serving plate and garnish with the scallions. **Serves 4 to 6.**

Boeuf Bourguignonne

Influenced by nouvelle cuisine, French chefs have lightened many of their classic dishes. This lean beef stew is inspired by a recipe from Alain Senderens, chef-owner of a three-star Parisian restaurant. The dish contains no added fat, but requires a good bottle of imported red Burgundy or domestic Pinot Noir and demi-glace, a concentrated meat broth, which can be found at some supermarkets and specialty stores or through the mail. If this dish seems extravagant, it's worth it.

1 large carrot, cut into 1-inch pieces

1 small onion, chopped

4 large garlic cloves, halved

¼ cup chopped fresh flat-leaf parsley

1 teaspoon juniper berries, crushed

1 teaspoon chopped fresh rosemary, or ½ teaspoon dried

½ teaspoon fresh thyme, or ¼ teaspoon dried

1 to 2 teaspoons fresh sage, or ¼ teaspoon crumbled dried

¼ teaspoon ground coriander

⅛ teaspoon cinnamon

⅛ teaspoon grated nutmeg

⅛ teaspoon black pepper

1 whole clove

1 bottle red Burgundy

2½ pounds lean chuck, cut into 16 cubes

1 cup demi-glace (jellied concentrated beef broth)

Four 2- x ½-inch strips orange zest

1 pound fresh fettuccine or ¾-inch-wide noodles

¼ cup chopped walnuts

In a large nonreactive bowl, combine the carrot, onion, garlic, parsley, juniper berries, rosemary, thyme, sage, coriander, cinnamon, nutmeg, pepper, and clove. Add the wine. Add the meat and stir well.

Cover and set in the refrigerator to marinate overnight or up to 24 hours.

Remove the meat from the marinade and place it in a soaked 3-quart clay pot. Strain the marinade, reserving 1¼ cups

Farmland, Burgundy

of the liquid and discarding the solids.

Add the reserved marinade and the demi-glace to the meat; the meat should be almost but not entirely covered by the liquid. Cover the pot and place it in a cold oven. Set the oven temperature to 450°F and cook for 1½ hours.

Add 2 of the strips of orange zest to the meat and cook for 15 minutes longer, or until the meat is almost fork-tender.

Meanwhile, cook the noodles in a large pot of salted boiling water; drain well. Cut the remaining 2 strips of orange zest into very thin julienne.

Place the noodles on 4 plates or in 4 shallow pasta bowls. Set 4 pieces of the cooked meat on each serving of noodles, and spoon over some of the cooking liquid. Sprinkle with the walnuts and the julienned orange zest and serve. **Serves 4.**

North African Pot Roast

Meat slowly simmered with beans makes a one-pot meal traditionally served after the Jewish Sabbath in many countries. In this Moroccan version, the pot holds chickpeas, sweet potatoes, and aromatic spices. The eggs cook gently and the spices give them a wonderful flavor. Sliced oranges drizzled with honey and cinnamon or rose water are a perfect dessert to follow this dish.

1 cup dried chickpeas, soaked overnight in water to cover & drained

1 medium onion, chopped

5 garlic cloves, chopped

½ cup golden raisins

½ teaspoon black pepper

½ teaspoon cinnamon

½ teaspoon mace

½ teaspoon turmeric

One 2 pound chuck or brisket of beef

2 sweet potatoes or yams, peeled, cut into ¾-inch slices

3 large eggs

3 to 4 cups chicken broth or water

Salt & black pepper

In a soaked 4-quart clay pot, combine the chickpeas, onion, garlic, raisins, pepper, cinnamon, mace, and turmeric. Set the meat on the chickpea mixture. Arrange the sweet potatoes and whole eggs around the meat. Add enough broth or water so the meat and eggs are almost covered.

Cover the pot and place it in a cold oven. Set the oven temperature to 300°F. Cook for about 4 hours, until the meat is tender, adding liquid as needed so the eggs are always at least partly submerged.

To serve, peel and quarter the eggs. Make a bed of chickpeas and yams on each plate and top with slices of beef and pieces of egg. **Serves 6.**

Red-Cooked Beef
with Star Anise & Scallions

*The Chinese call braising meat or poultry in a broth with soy sauce
"red cooking." Here the cooking broth is flavored with scallions, ginger, star anise,
and a touch of sugar. Try to use a naturally brewed Chinese soy sauce or one
from a natural food store. For a vegetarian version, use 2-inch cubes of tofu in
place of the meat and add chunks of carrot and daikon radish.*

2 tablespoons dark brown sugar

One 1-inch piece ginger,
   peeled & chopped

2 star anise

⅓ cup soy sauce

8 coffee beans (optional)

1 teaspoon Szechuan
   peppercorns (optional)

3 scallions, cut into
   3-inch lengths

2 garlic cloves, chopped

One 2 pound chuck or
   brisket of beef

In a medium-size saucepan, combine the sugar, ginger, star anise, and soy sauce. Add the coffee beans and peppercorns, if desired. Add 3 cups of water and bring to a boil. Reduce the heat, cover the pot, and simmer for 15 minutes.

In a soaked 3-quart clay pot, arrange the scallions to make a bed. Scatter the garlic over the scallions. Set the meat on top. Pour in the hot soy mixture. Cover the pot and place it in a cold oven. Set the oven temperature to 450°F and cook for 1½ hours, or until the meat is tender but still slightly chewy. Let the meat cool in the cooking liquid in the pot.

To serve, thinly slice the meat. Strain the cooking liquid. Serve the meat moistened with a bit of the cooking liquid. **Serves 6 to 8.**

Beef Braised in Ale

A good dark ale adds interesting depth of flavor to this carbonnade, a classic Belgian dish that is perfect for a large group. Any leftovers can be simmered in beef broth, with some chopped carrots and barley, to make a fortifying soup.

¼ cup canola oil

1½ pounds onions, halved & cut into ½-inch slices

One 3½-pound rump steak, well trimmed & cut into 1-inch slices

1 cup beef broth

2 tablespoons dark brown sugar

1 bay leaf

1 sprig fresh thyme, or 1 teaspoon dried

12 sprigs of fresh parsley

2 cups dark ale

In a medium-size heavy skillet, heat 2 tablespoons of the oil over medium-high heat. Add the onions and sauté for 12 to 15 minutes, until they are soft and golden. Transfer the onions to a soaked 4-quart clay pot.

In the same skillet, heat 1 tablespoon of the oil. Add half the meat, without crowding, and cook for about 8 minutes, turning once, until well browned on both sides. Add the meat to the onions.

Heat the remaining oil, and brown the remaining meat. Add it to the clay pot.

Pour the broth into the skillet and bring to a boil over high heat, scraping the pan to loosen the browned bits clinging to the bottom. Pour into the clay pot.

Sprinkle the sugar over the meat and onions. With kitchen string, tie together the bay leaf, thyme and parsley sprigs, and add to the pot. Pour the ale over the meat and onions. Cover the pot and place it in a cold oven. Set the oven temperature to 450°F and cook for 1 hour and 45 minutes, or until the meat is tender. **Serves 10.**

African Groundnut Stew

In Africa, peanuts are called groundnuts and are often pounded to a paste and used in soups, stews, and sauces. Here, peanut butter, tomatoes, and spices combine to make a creamy, rich sauce for this beef stew. Serve it with steamed collard greens or kale or a leafy green salad.

3 tablespoons canola oil

2 pounds lean beef chuck, cut into 1½-inch cubes

½ cup beef broth or water

1 medium onion, chopped

1 small green bell pepper, seeded & chopped

2 garlic cloves, minced

One ½-inch piece ginger, peeled & minced

½ cup smooth natural peanut butter

4 to 5 chopped canned plum tomatoes, plus enough of their juice to make 1 cup

½ teaspoon dried thyme

½ teaspoon cinnamon

¼ teaspoon ground allspice

Pinch of hot-pepper flakes

Juice of 1 lemon

In a large heavy skillet, heat 1 tablespoon of the oil over medium-high heat. Add half the beef and cook for about 12 minutes, turning occasionally, until well browned on all sides. Place the meat in a soaked 3-quart clay pot. Heat another tablespoon of the oil and brown the remaining meat. Add to the pot.

Add the broth to the skillet and bring to a boil, scraping up the browned bits from the bottom of the pan. Pour into a bowl and set aside.

Place the skillet over medium-high heat and heat the remaining oil. Add the onion, bell pepper, garlic, and ginger, and sauté for about 8 minutes, until the onions are soft but not browned. Add the sautéed vegetables to the clay pot.

Add the peanut butter, tomatoes, thyme, cinnamon, allspice, hot-pepper

Roasted peanuts

flakes, and lemon juice to the reserved broth, mixing until well combined. Pour this mixture over the meat and vegetables and stir to coat.

Cover the pot and place it in a cold oven. Set the oven temperature to 450°F and cook for 1 hour, or until the meat is tender and the sauce is thick and creamy. **Serves 4.**

Cotechino with Lentils

Northern Italians traditionally eat this garlicky sausage with lentils at the New Year to bring prosperity and luck. It is particularly good if you can get uncooked cotechino from an Italian salumeria, though cooked cotechino can be used.

One 1½-pound cotechino, preferably uncooked

1 pound green or brown lentils, picked over & rinsed

1 carrot, finely chopped

1 medium onion, finely chopped

1 stalk celery, finely chopped

2 garlic cloves, minced

2 cups chicken broth

Salt & black pepper

In a large bowl, soak the cotechino in water to cover for 1 to 2 hours.

Place the lentils in a soaked 3-quart clay pot. Stir in the carrot, onion, celery, and garlic. Add the broth and 1 cup of water. Cover the pot and place it in a cold oven. Set the oven temperature to 450°F and cook for 1 hour, until the lentils are soft but not mushy. (Check the lentils after 30 minutes, adding an additional cup of water if the liquid has dropped below the surface of the lentils.) Season with salt and pepper to taste.

Meanwhile, with a fork, pierce the cotechino in 8 to 10 places. Place the cotechino in a deep skillet and add enough water to cover. Cover the pan, bring the water to a simmer, and cook the sausage gently for 20 minutes if using cooked cotechino, 50 minutes if using uncooked.

Spoon the lentils onto a serving platter. Cut the sausage into ¾-inch slices and arrange over the lentils. **Serves 8.**

Pork Adobo

Adobo refers to a chile-infused marinade popular in Philippine and Mexican cooking. Traditionally, this marinade contains vinegar and garlic. Here, a blend of citrus juices and spices add subtler flavors. Using the shoulder end of the pork loin results in a moister roast. Freeze any leftover sauce to serve with pan-cooked pork chops or roasted chicken.

Marinade:

3 poblano chiles, roasted

3 large garlic cloves, chopped

1 medium onion, coarsely chopped

Juice of 1 lime

Juice of 1 orange

¼ cup plus 2 tablespoons cider vinegar

2 tablespoons ancho chile powder or regular chile powder

2 tablespoons soy sauce

1 tablespoon honey or dark brown sugar

½ teaspoon cinnamon

½ teaspoon ground cumin

½ teaspoon dried oregano

¼ teaspoon black pepper

One 4½-pound tied boneless pork loin, from the shoulder end

1 large onion, cut into 8 pieces

2 tablespoons peanut or canola oil

1 jalapeño pepper, seeded & finely chopped

To roast the chiles, place them directly over a gas flame or under the broiler. Cook until the skin darkens and blisters, turning frequently with tongs. Don't worry if the skin chars. Put the chiles in a brown paper bag to cool. With a small, sharp knife, peel off the skins. Seed and coarsely chop the chiles.

In a food processor, combine the poblano chiles, garlic, onion, lime and orange juices, ¼ cup of the vinegar, chile powder, soy sauce, honey, cinnamon, cumin, oregano, and pepper, and process to a liquid paste.

Pour the chile mixture into a 1-gallon plastic bag or other nonreactive container with a tight-fitting lid large enough to hold the pork roast. Add the meat and turn to coat well. Seal or cover tightly and refrigerate for 8 to 24 hours, turning the meat occasionally in the marinade.

Arrange the onion in a soaked 4-quart clay pot and set aside. In a large heavy skillet, heat the oil over medium-high heat. Add the pork and cook for about 10 minutes, until well browned on all sides, reducing the heat if necessary to avoid burning. Transfer the meat to the clay pot, using the onion pieces as a rack and placing the roast fat side up.

Remove the pan from the heat, pour the remaining vinegar into the hot pan, and scrape up all the browned bits. Add to the clay pot. Pour in the marinade. Cover the pot and place it in a cold oven. Set the oven temperature to 450°F and cook for 30 minutes.

Turn the roast over, spoon some of the sauce over the meat, cover, and cook until a quick-read thermometer inserted in the center registers 160°F, about 30 minutes. Remove the roast to a carving board and let rest for 15 to 20 minutes.

Meanwhile, discard the onion chunks and pour the liquid from the pot into a clear container. Skim off the fat. Stir in the jalapeño, and pour into a sauceboat.

Cut the meat into ¾-inch slices and serve with the sauce. **Serves 8.**

Pork Chops in Apricot-Kumquat Sauce

As this dish bakes, the fruits and spices melt into a rosy, sweet-tart sauce that complements the flavor of the pork. Boiled potatoes go well with this dish; use them to mop up every last bit of sauce.

4 kumquats

⅓ cup chopped dried Turkish apricots

1 medium onion, chopped

1 garlic clove, minced

1 tablespoon plus 1 teaspoon canola oil

6 center-cut pork chops, about ¾ inch thick

1 cup apple juice

3 tablespoons distilled white vinegar

2 tablespoons sugar

1 tablespoon tomato paste

¾ teaspoon ground ginger

¾ teaspoon ground cardamom

Halve the kumquats. Scoop out and discard the pulp. Cut the rinds crosswise into julienne. In a soaked 3-quart clay pot, combine the kumquat rinds, apricots, onion, and garlic.

In a medium-size heavy skillet, heat 2 teaspoons of the oil over medium-high heat. Add half of the chops and cook, turning once, for about 8 minutes, until browned on both sides. Transfer the chops to the clay pot, arranging them in one layer. Heat the remaining oil and brown the remaining chops. Add them to the clay pot in a second layer.

Pour ¾ cup of the apple juice into the skillet and bring to a boil, scraping the bottom of the pan with a wooden spoon to loosen any browned bits. Pour over the pork chops.

In a small bowl, blend the vinegar,

sugar, tomato paste, ginger, and cardamom with the remaining apple juice. Pour the mixture over the chops. Cover the pot and place it in a cold oven. Set the oven temperature to 450°F and cook for 1 hour, or until tender.

Place the chops on serving plates. Spoon some of the sauce and fruit over the chops. Pass the remaining sauce in a sauceboat or small bowl. **Serves 6.**

Lamb with Artichoke Hearts & Dill

Artichokes and baby lamb go well together, especially when enlivened Greek style with fresh lemon juice and dill. You can make this dish ahead and reheat it, using some of the sauce to moisten the meat and heating the rest of the sauce separately. Serve with noodles or rice.

1 lemon, halved, plus additional
    lemon juice to taste
2 large artichokes
3 tablespoons olive oil
4 lamb shanks (¾ to 1 pound
    each), well trimmed
½ cup dry white wine

1 medium onion, chopped
2 garlic cloves, chopped
1 cup chicken broth
½ cup plus 2 tablespoons
    minced fresh dill
Salt & black pepper

Fill a small bowl with cold water. Squeeze in the juice from half of the lemon and add the squeezed lemon half.

To trim and core the artichokes, break off the outer leaves of 1 of the artichokes until you reach the light green leaves. Cut off the top of the artichoke far enough down so you can see the feathery tips of the choke. Cut off the stem flush with the bottom of the artichoke and discard. Halve the artichoke length-wise. Using a melon baller or spoon, scoop out the choke. With a small knife, trim off and discard all the remaining leaves and the tough parts from the arti-choke bottom. Cut the artichoke bottom into 3 to 4 wedges and put them in the acidulated water. Repeat with the remaining artichoke.

In a large skillet, heat 2 tablespoons of the oil over medium-high heat. Add the lamb and cook, turning occasionally, for about 15 minutes, until well browned all over. Place the shanks in one layer in a soaked 4-quart clay pot.

Pour the wine into the skillet, remove the pan from the heat, and, using a wooden spoon, scrape up the browned bits from the bottom of the pan. Pour over the lamb shanks. Wipe out the pan with a paper towel and return it to the stove.

Heat the remaining oil in the skillet over medium-high heat. Add the onion and garlic, and sauté for 3 to 4 minutes, until the onion is soft. Add to the lamb.

Pour the broth and 1 cup of water over the lamb. Cover the pot and place it in a cold oven. Set the oven temperature to 450°F and cook for 20 minutes.

Reduce the oven temperature to 350°F and cook for 45 minutes more.

Squeeze the juice from the remaining lemon and add it to the lamb along with the artichoke hearts and ½ cup of the dill. Mix to blend. Cover the pot and cook for about 15 minutes, until the lamb is browned and very tender and the artichokes are fork-tender.

Transfer the lamb and artichoke hearts to a warm serving platter and cover to keep warm. Pour the liquid from the clay pot into a medium-size saucepan. Bring to a boil and boil until it is reduced by half, about 5 minutes. Season with salt and pepper to taste. Add more lemon juice, if you wish. Stir in the remaining dill. Pour the sauce into a sauceboat. Serve the lamb, passing the sauce. **Serves 4.**

Gigot of Lamb with Garlic

Slivers of garlic tucked into this French-style roast lamb perfume it with glorious flavor. New potatoes and pale green French flageolet beans would be perfect accompaniments.

One 6- to 7-pound shank-end
    leg of lamb (about
    4½ pounds trimmed)

2 large garlic cloves, cut
    into thin slivers

1 large potato, cut into
    1-inch cubes

1 large carrot, cut into
    1-inch slices

½ cup chicken or
    vegetable broth

Using a sharp paring knife, make about 20 ¼-inch-deep slits in the lamb. Press a sliver of garlic into each slit.

Arrange the potato and carrot in a soaked 3-quart clay pot to form a rack for the meat. Place the lamb on the vegetables. Pour in the broth. Cover the pot and place it in a cold oven. Set the oven temperature to 450°F and cook for 50 minutes.

Uncover the pot and cook for 10 to 15 minutes longer, until the lamb is browned and a thermometer inserted into the center of the meat, away from the bone, registers 120°F. Place the lamb on a platter and let it sit for 15 minutes to allow the juices to settle. (The meat will continue cooking as it sits.)

Pour the pan juices into a small bowl or sauceboat and discard the vegetables. Skim off the fat. Slice the lamb and serve it accompanied by the pan juices. **Serves 6.**

Portuguese Peas

*Bright green peas, fresh cilantro, spicy sausage, and oven-poached eggs give
this colorful dish its Portuguese character. Serve it directly from
its earthenware casserole with thick, buttered slices of toasted Portuguese
sweet bread or challah for a brunch or light supper.*

4 cups fresh or frozen
   green peas

I small onion, finely chopped

I stalk celery, finely chopped

I ounce chorizo or pepperoni
   sausage, sliced as thinly as
   possible

½ small roasted red bell
   pepper or pimiento (p. 46),
   cut into ¼-inch strips

I cup chicken broth

I tablespoon minced
   fresh flat-leaf parsley

I tablespoon minced
   fresh cilantro

4 large eggs, in their shells

½ teaspoon sweet paprika

Salt & black pepper

Preheat the oven to 400°F.

Put the peas in a 12¼-inch cazuela or other shallow heatproof dish. Stir in the onion and celery. Arrange the sausage and bell pepper strips on top. Pour in the broth. Cover the cazuela loosely with aluminum foil, place it in the oven, and bake for 20 minutes, or until the peas are hot.

Remove the cazuela from the oven and sprinkle the parsley and cilantro over the vegetables.

Break 1 egg into a small dish. Gently slide it onto the vegetables. Repeat with the remaining eggs, placing them so they do not touch each other.

Sprinkle the paprika and the salt and pepper to taste over the eggs. Bake, uncovered, for 5 to 8 minutes, until the egg whites are firm and the yolks are set. Serve immediately. **Serves 4.**

Eight-Treasure Sand Pot Casserole

This healthy Chinese stew, served in its cozy clay pot, combines crisp stir-fried vegetables with shining noodles in an intense, mushroom-rich sauce. Every step in this recipe is simple, and each of the ingredients is beautiful.

4 large dried black mushrooms

12 dried lily buds

6 small dried tree ear mushrooms

One 1¾-ounce package bean thread noodles

2 cups chicken broth

3 scallions (white & tender green parts), cut into 2-inch lengths

One 1-inch piece ginger, peeled & cut into 4 slices

½ teaspoon sugar

2 tablespoons dry sherry

½ cup peanut oil

8 ounces firm tofu, cut into 12 cubes

1 large carrot, cut into 12 diagonal slices

¼ cup bamboo shoots, cut lengthwise into ¼-inch strips

One ½-pound wedge Napa cabbage, cut lengthwise into ½-inch strips

12 snow peas, trimmed

4 fresh water chestnuts, peeled & sliced, or ¼ cup canned sliced water chestnuts, rinsed

2 tablespoons cornstarch

1 tablespoon soy sauce

1 tablespoon rice vinegar

½ teaspoon Asian sesame oil

Salt

In a bowl, soak the black mushrooms in 1 cup hot tap water for about 20 minutes, until soft. (Do not use boiling water; it draws off too much flavor.)

In separate bowls, soak the lily buds and the tree ears in hot tap water for about 20 minutes, until soft. In another bowl, cover the bean thread

noodles with warm water and soak for 20 minutes.

Drain the black mushrooms, strain and reserve ½ cup of the soaking water, and squeeze to remove excess water. Cut the mushrooms into ⅜-inch strips and set aside. Drain the lily buds, squeezing to remove excess water. Trim off any hard ends. Tear each bud lengthwise into 2 to 3 strips and set aside. Drain the tree ears. Cut away any hard bits and cut each one into 2 to 3 pieces. Set aside. Drain the bean thread noodles and set aside.

In a large sand pot (p. 8) or flameproof casserole, combine the mushroom soaking water, broth, scallions, ginger, sugar, and sherry. If using a sand pot, set on a flame-tamer over medium-high heat. If using a flameproof casserole, a flame-tamer is unnecessary. Cover and bring to a simmer; this may take 15 to 20 minutes because clay is slow to heat. Cook for 15 minutes.

In a wok, heat the peanut oil over high heat. Add the tofu and stir-fry until golden and crisp on all sides. With a slotted spoon, remove the tofu and drain on paper towels.

Discard all but 1 tablespoon of the oil from the wok. Add the carrot, bamboo shoots, and cabbage, and stir-fry for 3 minutes, or until the cabbage is slightly wilted. Add the stir-fried vegetables to the sand pot. Toss the snow peas into the wok and stir-fry for 30 seconds, just until they turn bright green. Add to the sand pot. Add the black mushrooms, lily buds, tree ears, bean thread noodles, and water chestnuts.

In a small bowl, blend the cornstarch with the soy sauce and 2 tablespoons of cold water. Stir this mixture into the sand pot. Using a wok spatula, stir until the liquid thickens to the consistency of a sauce. The rounded shape of the spatula will help ensure no lumps form on the bottom of the pot. Stir in the vinegar, sesame oil, and salt to taste. Add the tofu. Immediately bring the sand pot to the table, and ladle the stew into 4 individual bowls. **Serves 4.**

Red Peppers Stuffed with Millet & Corn

*Few Americans are familiar with millet, although this light grain
is a staple food in much of the world. Combined with corn and packed into
sweet red peppers, it makes a satisfying vegetarian main course,
bright with the flavors of mint and fresh lemon. The dish can be assembled
ahead, then cooked at your convenience.*

1½ cups vegetable broth

½ cup millet

1 cup fresh, canned, or
   thawed frozen corn

1 medium onion, finely chopped

1 stalk celery, finely chopped

¼ cup chopped walnuts

1 tablespoon minced shallots

1 tablespoon chopped fresh
   mint, or 1 teaspoon dried

1½ teaspoons minced fresh
   oregano, or ½ teaspoon dried

2 teaspoons grated lemon zest

Salt & black pepper

4 medium red bell peppers

¼ cup extra-virgin olive oil

2 tablespoons fresh lemon juice

In a medium-size saucepan, bring the broth to a boil. Add the millet, cover, and cook for 20 minutes, or until tender. Transfer to a medium-size bowl and let cool.

Using a fork, fluff the millet. With the fork, stir in the corn, onion, celery, walnuts, shallots, mint, oregano, and lemon zest. Season with the salt and pepper to taste.

Cut the tops off the bell peppers. Remove the seeds and ribs. If necessary, trim the bottoms of the peppers so they stand upright, taking care not to pierce through the peppers. Pack the millet mixture into the peppers. Brush

the top of the filling lightly with some of the oil.

Set the peppers in a soaked 3-quart clay pot. Pour in 1 cup of water. Cover the pot and place it in a cold oven. Set the oven temperature to 450°F and cook for 30 minutes. Uncover the peppers, reduce the temperature to 375°F, and cook for 15 minutes longer, or until the peppers are soft but not collapsing.

Just before serving, in a small bowl, whisk the remaining oil with the lemon juice. Season with salt and pepper to taste.

Spoon the dressing over the peppers, and serve warm or at room temperature. **Serves 4.**

Stuffed Onions Agrodolce

The Italian antipasto table offers many stuffed vegetables. These tender sweet and sour onions may be the best of all. Serve as a first course, or as a light meatless main course, accompanied by a salad of arugula and radicchio, and crusty bread.

4 medium onions

I cup cooked brown rice

3 large plum tomatoes, 2 seeded & diced, I cut into 4 slices

2 tablespoons dried currants

½ teaspoon dried oregano

2 tablespoons red wine vinegar

⅔ cup chicken broth

2 tablespoons extra-virgin olive oil

Peel the onions. Cut off the tops at the point where the sides start to curve in toward the top. Cook the onions in a large pot of boiling water for 2 minutes. With a slotted spoon, remove the onions from the pot.

When the onions are cool enough to handle, use a melon baller to scoop out the flesh, leaving a shell 2 layers thick.

In a bowl, combine the rice, the diced tomatoes, currants, oregano, and vinegar. Pack the mixture into the onions.

Place the onions in a soaked 3-quart clay pot, and pour in the broth. Place 1 slice of the tomato on top of each onion. Drizzle the oil over the onions. Cover the pot and place it in a cold oven. Set the oven temperature to 450°F and cook for 50 minutes, or until the onions are soft but not mushy when pierced with a knife.

Place the onions on a plate. Pour the liquid from the clay pot into a small saucepan. Bring to a boil over high heat and boil until reduced to ¼ cup. Spoon the liquid over the onions. Serve warm or at room temperature. **Serves 4.**

Black & White Chipotle Chili

The beans in this chili have the creamy texture
typical of legumes baked in clay. Chipotle and New Mexico chiles,
plus lots of fresh cilantro, give the chili so much flavor
that no one will not notice the meat is missing. Serve with
chopped red onions and sour cream, if desired.

1 pound dried black turtle beans, picked over & rinsed

1 pound dried white kidney beans, picked over & rinsed

3 dried chipotle chiles

1 tablespoon ground cumin

1 tablespoon dried oregano

1 tablespoon sweet paprika

½ teaspoon cayenne

3 tablespoons canola oil

2 cups chopped onions

2 cups chopped green bell peppers

8 garlic cloves, chopped

2 bay leaves

1 tablespoon New Mexico chili powder

1 cup chopped fresh cilantro

2 pounds plum tomatoes, halved, seeded & chopped

1 tablespoon salt

Soak the black and white beans separately in water to cover for at least 8 hours, or overnight. Or use the Quick-Soak Method (p. 79). (Do not combine the beans or the black ones will darken the white ones.)

In a small bowl, soak the chipotles in ½ cup of warm water for about 30 minutes, until soft. Drain, reserving the soaking water.

In a medium-size heavy skillet, toast the cumin, oregano, paprika, and cayenne over medium-high heat for 1 minute, or until just fragrant. Immediately stir in the oil. Add the onions, bell peppers, and garlic, and sauté for about 10 minutes, until the onions are soft. Remove from the heat.

In a soaked 4-quart clay pot, combine

Chiles drying, Santa Fe, New Mexico

the beans with the onion mixture. Add the bay leaves and the reserved chipotle soaking water. Add enough water to come to just below the surface of the beans. Cover the pot and place it in a cold oven. Set the oven temperature to 450°F and cook for 45 minutes.

Stir the chipotles, chili powder, cilantro, and tomatoes into the chili. Add water if needed to come just below the surface of the beans. Cook the chili for 45 minutes longer, or until the beans are soft. Remove the bay leaves and stir in the salt. **Serves 12 to 15.**

Green Beans
with Tomatoes & Feta Cheese

*Serve these beans as a light side dish, warm or at room temperature,
to accompany grilled lamb chops. Try to find Greek or Bulgarian feta, which
have a tangier flavor than other varieties.*

1 pound green beans, trimmed

3 plum tomatoes, cut into
    ¾-inch slices

1 garlic clove, minced

¼ teaspoon dried oregano

½ teaspoon salt

¼ teaspoon black pepper

½ cup chicken or
    vegetable broth

½ cup crumbled Greek or
    Bulgarian feta cheese

2 tablespoons fresh lemon juice

1 tablespoon extra-virgin
    olive oil

2 tablespoons chopped fresh
    flat-leaf parsley, for garnish

Place the beans in a soaked 3-quart clay pot. Top with the tomatoes. Sprinkle with the garlic, oregano, salt, and pepper. Pour in the broth. Top with the crumbled feta. Cover the clay pot and place it in a cold oven. Set the oven temperature to 450°F and cook for 40 minutes, or until the beans are just al dente.

With a slotted spoon, transfer the vegetables and cheese to a serving plate. Drizzle with the lemon juice and oil. Sprinkle with the parsley just before serving. **Serves 4.**

Braised Red Cabbage
with Cranberries

*This vibrant version of a popular classic pairs nicely with game,
pot roast, or Beef Braised in Ale (p. 41). It's a dish that reheats well. In fact,
it's even better made the day before you plan to serve it.*

2 tablespoons unsalted butter

One 2 to 2½ pound
red cabbage, quartered,
cored & cut into
½-inch strips

1½ cups cranberries,
fresh or frozen

¼ cup raspberry or
wildflower honey

1 cup raspberry-apple juice

¾ teaspoon ground cardamom

¼ cup red wine vinegar

½ teaspoon salt

¼ teaspoon black pepper

In a medium-size heavy skillet, melt 1 tablespoon of the butter over medium-high heat. Add half the cabbage and sauté for 5 minutes, or until wilted. Transfer the cabbage to a soaked 3-quart clay pot. Melt the remaining butter and wilt the remaining cabbage. Add it to the clay pot.

Add the cranberries, honey, juice, cardamom, vinegar, salt, and pepper, and mix gently to blend. Cover the pot and place it in a cold oven. Set the oven temperature to 425°F and cook for 45 minutes, or until the cabbage is tender but not mushy. With a slotted spoon, remove the cabbage to a serving dish. (Reserve some of the cooking liquid for reheating the cabbage if necessary). **Serves 6 to 8.**

Romanian Gvetch

*As a child, I loved it when my grandmother made a big pot
of gvetch, a kind of Eastern European ratatouille, because it was so
sweet from the parsnips and sweet potatoes.*

1 medium sweet potato, peeled
& cut into 1-inch cubes

1 medium white potato, peeled
& cut into 1-inch cubes

1 medium onion, finely chopped

1 medium carrot, cut into
¾-inch slices

1 small eggplant, cut into
1-inch cubes

1 small parsnip, cut into
¾-inch slices

1 small zucchini, cut into
¾-inch slices

1 small green bell pepper,
seeded & cut into
1-inch pieces

1 small red bell pepper, seeded
& cut into 1-inch pieces

½ small cauliflower, separated
into florets

½ pound mushrooms,
stemmed & quartered

¼ pound green beans, trimmed

½ cup dry white wine

2 tablespoons tomato paste

2 teaspoons sweet paprika

½ teaspoon dried thyme

1½ cups chicken broth

1 bay leaf

½ cup chopped fresh
flat-leaf parsley

In a soaked 4-quart clay pot, combine all the vegetables.

In a bowl, stir together the wine, tomato paste, paprika, and thyme. Mix in the broth. Pour the mixture over the vegetables and add the bay leaf. Sprinkle with the parsley. Cover the pot and place it in a cold oven. Set the oven temperature to 450°F and cook for 1 hour. Serve with a crusty bread, such as French Bâtard (p. 84). **Serves 12.**

Spinach Tian

Because of its simplicity, a tian, a bread-crumb-topped casserole of vegetables braised in olive oil, is best made from farm-fresh ingredients and good, fruity olive oil. Enjoy this Provençal favorite with Pork Chops in Apricot-Kumquat Sauce (p. 48).

3 tablespoons extra-virgin
　olive oil

1½ pounds fresh spinach

1 large shallot, minced

½ teaspoon finely chopped fresh
　rosemary, or ¼ teaspoon
　crushed dried

¾ teaspoon salt

Black pepper

3 tablespoons fresh
　bread crumbs

2 tablespoons grated
　Parmesan cheese

Preheat the oven to 375°F. Grease a tian, 8½-inch cazuela, or heatproof dish with 1 tablespoon of the oil and set aside.

Stem the spinach, wash thoroughly, and drain throughly. Coarsely chop the spinach and put it in a large bowl.

Toss the spinach well with the remaining olive oil, the shallot, rosemary, and salt and pepper to taste. Pack the mixture into the tian.

In a small bowl, combine the bread crumbs and cheese. Sprinkle evenly over the spinach.

Bake for about 30 minutes, until the spinach is soft and the bread crumbs are golden brown. **Serves 4.**

Potato Gratin

Slice the potatoes as thinly as possible and be generous with the butter in this creamy, luscious dish. If you have cooking parchment paper, cut a piece to fit the bottom of your clay pot to help ease the cake onto a serving plate.

4 tablespoons unsalted
   butter, melted
2½ pounds baking potatoes,
   peeled & sliced as thinly
   as possible

½ small onion, very thinly sliced
Salt & black pepper

Brush the bottom of a soaked 3-quart clay pot with 1 tablespoon of the melted butter. Cover the bottom of the pot with overlapping slices of potato, arranging them like roof tiles.

Arrange an overlapping ring of potato slices around the edge of the clay pot so that the slices curve about a third of the way up the sides and overlap the slices on the bottom to form a shell. Brush the potatoes with another tablespoon of melted butter, holding the slices gently in place with your fingers if necessary. Sprinkle with half the onion, separating it into individual strips. Season with salt and pepper to taste.

Layer half the remaining sliced potatoes in the "shell." Brush with half the remaining melted butter. Sprinkle with the remaining onion and salt and pepper to taste. Cover with the remaining sliced potatoes. Brush with the remaining melted butter, and season with salt and pepper to taste.

Cut a piece of aluminum foil the length of the clay pot and fold it in half lengthwise. Press the foil over the potatoes, letting the sides of the foil lie against the insides of the pot.

Place the uncovered pot in a cold oven. Set the oven temperature to 425°F and bake for 45 to 50 minutes, until the

Potato fields, southern Idaho

potatoes feel tender when a knife is inserted into the center of the cake and the sides are golden brown.

Discard the foil. Place an oval serving platter over the clay pot and invert the potatoes onto the serving platter. Serve immediately. **Serves 6.**

Baked Acorn Squash
with Cranberries

*The squash and cranberries both bake and steam inside
the moist clay pot, keeping their vibrant colors
while the sweet and tart flavors of the ingredients marry.
Serve this with roasted chicken or turkey.*

2 small acorn squash, halved
    lengthwise & seeded
¼ cup maple syrup
1½ cups fresh or
    frozen cranberries

½ teaspoon ground ginger
½ teaspoon ground allspice
2 tablespoons unsalted butter
1 cup apple juice

Place the squash cut side up in a soaked 3-quart clay pot. Brush with 2 tablespoons of the maple syrup.

In a bowl, combine the cranberries, ginger, allspice, and the remaining maple syrup. Fill the squash halves with the berry mixture. Cut the butter into thin chips and dot it over the squash. Pour the apple juice into the pot. Cover the pot and place it in a cold oven. Set the oven temperature to 450°F and cook for 45 minutes, or until the squash is soft when pierced with a knife. Serve immediately. **Serves 4.**

Baked Risotto

Plump Italian rice baked in an open earthenware casserole absorbs even more flavor than when prepared in a standard risotto. This braising also requires less tending; you'll have time to prepare a green salad or simple veal dish while giving the rice an occasional stir. Barolo is the wine of choice for this dish but it is costly. If you replace it with a dry white, then change the beef broth to a chicken broth.

3 cups beef broth or canned low-sodium broth

2 tablespoons olive oil

1 small onion, finely chopped

1½ cups Arborio rice

¼ cup minced prosciutto (1 ounce)

½ cup Barolo wine

¼ cup grated Parmesan cheese

Salt & black pepper

Preheat the oven to 400°F.

In a saucepan, bring the broth almost to a boil. Turn off the heat, cover, and set aside.

In a medium-size skillet, heat the oil over medium-high heat. Add the onion and sauté for 3 to 4 minutes, until soft. Add the rice and stir until well coated with oil. Stir in the prosciutto. Add 2 cups of the hot broth and bring to a boil. Transfer the rice to a 12¼-inch cazuela.

Place the cazuela in the oven and cook for 15 minutes. Stir in the wine and cook for 5 minutes, or until the rice has absorbed most of the liquid. Stir in ½ cup of the broth and cook for about 5 minutes, or until the rice has absorbed most of the liquid. Stir in the remaining broth and cook for about 5 minutes longer, or until the rice is al dente but still slightly soupy.

Stir the Parmesan into the rice. Season with salt and pepper to taste and serve. **Serves 4.**

Lemon Orzo

Orzo is a rice-shaped pasta often used in Greek recipes. Simmering this pasta in the oven in an open earthenware casserole gives it the creamy texture reminiscent of risotto. The zesty flavor of this dish goes perfectly with Lamb with Artichoke Hearts & Dill (p. 50) or with baked salmon, snapper, or bass.

1 tablespoon olive oil

1 small onion, finely chopped

1 cup orzo

2 cups chicken broth or one 13¾-ounce can chicken broth

Grated zest & juice of 1 lemon

1 teaspoon minced fresh oregano, or ½ teaspoon dried

Black pepper

¼ cup grated Parmesan cheese

Salt

Preheat the oven to 400°F.

In a skillet, heat the oil over medium-high heat. Add the onion and sauté for about 4 minutes, until soft. Add the orzo and stir to coat with the oil. Transfer the onion and orzo to a 12¼-inch cazuela.

Pour the broth into the skillet. Add enough water to make 3 cups liquid and bring to a boil. Pour the liquid into the cazuela. Stir in the lemon zest, juice, oregano, and pepper to taste.

Bake for 20 minutes, or until the orzo is creamy and al dente. Stir in the Parmesan cheese and season with salt and pepper to taste. Serve immediately. **Serves 4.**

Ginger Baked Beans

The shape of the traditional clay bean pot is designed to keep the beans moist and to let a crust form over them as they slowly bake. If you don't have a bean pot, make the beans, covered, in a cast-iron Dutch oven. The salt pork can be omitted, but it adds to the rich flavor of the beans.

1 pound dried navy beans, picked over & rinsed

½ cup tomato sauce

⅓ cup unsulphured molasses

2 tablespoons dark brown sugar

2 tablespoons maple syrup

2 teaspoons ground mustard

1½ teaspoons ground ginger

1 small onion

2 whole cloves

2 ounces salt pork, in 1 piece, rinsed & dried

Soak the beans in water to cover for 6 to 8 hours, or use the Quick-Soak Method (see below).

Preheat the oven to 400°F. Drain the beans and place the beans in a 2½-quart glazed bean pot or covered casserole.

In a small saucepan, combine the tomato sauce, molasses, sugar, maple syrup, mustard, and ginger. Bring to a simmer and cook, stirring, for about 4 minutes, or until the sugar has dissolved. Pour the mixture over the beans. Add 2 cups of water and stir to blend.

Cut the onion in half lengthwise, stopping just above the roots so the halves remain attached. Turn the onion 90 degrees and repeat. Stick the cloves into the onion. Add the onion to the bean pot (it will float).

With a sharp knife, score the skin of the salt pork, making 2 to 3 cuts diagonally in each direction. Place the salt pork, fat side down, in the bean pot.

Bake for 1 hour. Reduce the temperature to 250°F and continue baking for 5 to 6 hours, until the beans are soft.

To keep the beans from drying out, add about 3 cups of water if needed. Serve hot. **Serves 8 to 10.**

Quick-Soak Method: Place the beans in a large saucepan with 8 cups of water. Cover the pot and bring to a boil. Cook for 2 minutes, then remove the pot from the heat and let sit, covered, for 1 hour. Drain the beans.

Dal with Tomato Confit

Dal *refers both to the cooked dish and to the many kinds of dried lentils, split peas, and mung beans Indian cooks use. Since these protein-rich dishes are served at almost every meal, there are an infinite variety of recipes for them, from all parts of India. Here cooking reduces red lentils to a golden purée. Mixed with the jam-like spicy tomato confit, this dal can be a main course or a side dish with fish or chicken.*

1½ cups dried red lentils, picked over & rinsed

3 tablespoons olive oil

1 medium onion, chopped

3 garlic cloves, chopped

One 1-inch piece ginger, peeled & finely chopped

2 jalapeño or *serrano* chiles, seeded & finely chopped

2 teaspoons black mustard seeds (optional)

½ teaspoon cinnamon

½ teaspoon ground coriander

½ teaspoon ground cumin

¼ teaspoon black pepper

¼ teaspoon fennel seed

⅛ teaspoon ground cardamom

⅛ teaspoon ground cloves

4 to 5 plum tomatoes, seeded & chopped (1 cup)

Juice of 1 orange

1 tablespoon chopped fresh cilantro

1 tablespoon unsalted butter

In a soaked 3-quart clay pot, combine the lentils and 4 cups of water. Cover the pot and place it in a cold oven. Set the oven temperature to 450°F and cook for 30 to 40 minutes, until the lentils are soft.

Check the lentils by stirring; they should be soft and mushy. Transfer to a bowl.

Meanwhile, heat the oil in a heavy skillet over medium-high heat. Add the onion and cook, stirring occasionally, for

about 15 minutes, until well browned. Stir in the garlic, ginger, and jalapeños. Add the spices and stir to blend. Stir in the tomatoes, orange juice, and cilantro. Bring to a simmer and cook for 20 to 25 minutes, until the tomatoes are very soft. Stir in the butter.

Spoon the tomato confit over the dal and serve. **Serves 4 to 6.**

Moroccan Semolina Bread

*In Morocco, everyone eats with their hands, using pieces of bread to scoop up
each mouthful and soak up plenty of flavorful juices. The dense,
chewy texture and thick, crisp crust of this bread are ideal for this. Try serving
with Chicken Tagine with Green Olives & Preserved Lemon (p. 32).*

2 tablespoons cornmeal

1½ teaspoons active dry yeast

1 cup lukewarm water

2 tablespoons olive oil

1 teaspoon cumin seeds

1 teaspoon salt

½ cup all-purpose flour

¼ cup rye flour

2 to 2¼ cups semolina flour

2 teaspoons sesame seeds

Grease the round bottom of a covered stoneware bread baker with a little oil, and sprinkle with the cornmeal.

In a large bowl, dissolve the yeast in the water. Stir in the the oil, cumin seeds, and salt. With a wooden spoon, stir in the all-purpose and rye flours, along with enough of the semolina flour to make a very stiff dough.

Turn the dough out onto a work surface dusted with about 2 tablespoons semolina flour. Begin to knead the dough, incorporating small amounts of the remaining semolina flour. Use only as much as needed to produce a smooth and elastic dough. Continue to knead for about 10 minutes.

Shape the dough into a round loaf and place it on the bottom of the prepared baker. Gently brush about 1 teaspoon of water over the surface of the dough. Sprinkle on the sesame seeds and gently pat them to adhere. Place the dome cover of the baker on top, and set aside in a warm, draft-free place for about 30 minutes, until doubled in bulk.

Meanwhile, preheat the oven to 400°F. Bake for 35 minutes. Uncover and

Open air bread baking, Morocco

bake an additional 10 to 12 minutes, until the crust is a nice golden brown. The bread is done when it sounds hollow when tapped on the bottom. Remove and let cool on a wire rack. Serve the loaf whole and let diners break off pieces. **Makes 1 loaf.**

French Bâtard

*Baking in clay ensures this classic bread has a strong
crust and a chewy, moist center, rather like a sourdough bread.
As the bread cools, the crust may crackle and shatter
somewhat; that is normal for breads baked in this type of pan.*

1 (¼-ounce) package active
    dry yeast
⅓ cup plus 1¼ cups warm water
    (80°F to 90°F)

4 to 5 cups all-purpose flour
2¼ teaspoons coarse salt
1 to 2 tablespoons vegetable oil
2 tablespoons cornmeal

In the bowl of a heavy-duty electric mixer, stir the yeast into the ⅓ cup warm water. Let sit for a few minutes to dissolve. Stir to be sure the yeast is completely dissolved. Add 4 cups of the flour, then the salt. Pour in the remaining warm water. Using the dough hook, mix until the dough pulls cleanly away from the side of the bowl and forms a smooth mass around the dough hook, adding more flour if necessary.

Scrape the dough onto a lightly floured work surface. Knead until elastic and satiny, adding more flour if necessary.

Place the dough in a large oiled bowl.

Cover it with plastic wrap and a kitchen towel. Let rise in a warm, draft-free place for about 1½ hours, or until tripled in bulk.

Scrape the dough out onto a floured work surface and knead it to remove any air bubbles. (At this point, the dough can be set in the bowl, covered with plastic wrap, and refrigerated overnight, or wrapped and frozen.)

Return the dough to the bowl, and cover it with plastic wrap and the towel. Let rise in a warm, draft-free place for about 30 minutes, until doubled in bulk.

Place the top of the rectangular clay bread baker in the sink, with the handle

in the drain hole, and fill it with warm water. Grease the inside of the bottom of the clay baker with the oil and sprinkle it with the cornmeal.

Scrape the dough out onto a lightly floured work surface and shape it into a loaf to fit the baker. Set the dough in the bottom of the baker. Place the pan, uncovered, in a warm, draft-free place for about 30 minutes, until doubled in bulk.

Preheat the oven to 400°F. Slash the top of the loaf diagonally in 4 or 5 places. Brush it with water. Drain the top of the clay baker and cover and bake the bread for 45 minutes. Uncover and bake for 5 to 10 minutes longer, until the top and sides are nicely colored and the loaf sounds hollow when tapped on the bottom.

Remove the bread from the clay baker and transfer to a rack to cool. **Makes 1 loaf.**

Ham & Jalapeño Corn Bread

You could almost make a meal of this corn bread. In fact,
a wedge of it, halved, generously buttered, and sandwiching a slice
of Monterey Jack cheese, makes a perfect breakfast or snack.

1 cup yellow cornmeal

1 cup all-purpose flour

3 tablespoons sugar

1 teaspoon baking powder

1 teaspoon baking soda

½ teaspoon salt

1 large egg

1 cup buttermilk

3 tablespoons corn or canola oil

¼ cup finely minced Smithfield ham or prosciutto (1 ounce)

1 or 2 jalapeño peppers, roasted (p.46), peeled, seeded & minced

Preheat the oven to 425°F. Grease an 8½-inch cazuela with butter.

In a medium-size bowl, sift together the cornmeal, flour, sugar, baking powder, baking soda, and salt.

In a medium-size bowl, beat the egg. Stir in the buttermilk, oil, ham, and jalapeño.

Using a fork, mix the wet ingredients into the dry until well blended. Scrape the batter into the cazuela.

Bake for 25 minutes, or until the top of the bread is golden brown and crusty, and a knife inserted in the center comes out clean. Turn the corn bread out onto a rack. Reinvert it onto a serving plate. Cut into wedges and serve hot. **Serves 8.**

Pears in Sauternes

In this simple yet elegant dessert, which glows with golden color and the exquisite flavor of the wine, the pears both steam and poach, making them meltingly tender. Daizy Doigny is a good and affordably priced Sauternes frequently available in half-bottles. You will have pear syrup left over: Save it to spoon over other fruit or vanilla ice cream, or mix with club soda for a divine spritzer.

1⅔ cups Sauternes

⅓ cup sugar

Three 1 × ½-inch strips lemon zest

1 bay leaf

1 vanilla bean

4 Bartlett pears

Pour the wine into a soaked 3-quart clay pot. Add the sugar, lemon zest, and bay leaf.

Lay the vanilla bean on a work surface. With the tip of a small, sharp knife, slit the vanilla bean open lengthwise. With the knife, scrape out the seeds and add them to the clay pot. Don't worry if the seeds cling together.

Peel the pears, leaving the stems intact. Using a melon baller, core the pears by scooping the core out from the bottom.

Stand the pears in the clay pot. Cover the pot and place it in a cold oven. Set the oven temperature to 425°F and bake for 30 minutes, or until the pears are soft when pierced with a knife.

Place the pears on 4 dessert plates. Pour the cooking liquid into a small saucepan. Bring to a boil over high heat and boil for 5 to 8 minutes, until the liquid is slightly syrupy. Spoon this syrup over the pears and serve. Or let the pears and the syrup cool to room temperature before pouring the syrup over the pears and serving. **Serves 4.**

Honey-Baked Spiced Quinces

Quinces look like rustic apples. Cooked, they taste like apples with overtones of pear and pineapple. When quinces are not available, use a firm apple, such as Rome Beauty, Mutsu, or Crispin. While apples won't blush as quinces do, you'll still get a wonderfully spicy fruit dessert that is great served warm, topped with a scoop of vanilla ice cream.

3 quinces or firm apples, peeled, quartered & cored

½ cup frozen apple juice concentrate, thawed

¼ cup wildflower or other mild honey

¼ teaspoon ground allspice

¼ teaspoon ground cardamom

¼ teaspoon ground ginger

Vanilla ice cream (optional)

In a soaked 3-quart clay pot, place the quinces or apples in one layer. Add the juice concentrate and honey. Add the allspice, cardamom, and ginger, sprinkling the spices between the wedges of fruit. Cover the pot and place it in a cold oven. Set the oven temperature to 425°F. Bake until the fruit is soft when pierced with a sharp knife but still holds its shape, 45 to 60 minutes for quinces, 35 to 45 minutes for apples. When done, quinces will be a rosy golden color, apples will look somewhat darkened and glazed. The liquid in the pot will have reduced to a syrup.

Divide the fruit among 4 bowls. Top with a small scoop of vanilla ice cream, if desired. Serve warm. **Serves 4.**

Peach-Blackberry Crumple

*The clear, true flavors of the juicy peaches and berries bubbling under
a crisp filo crust come through because no thickening is used in
this luscious deep-dish dessert. If you wish to cut down on fat, omit the
butter in the filling; you'll still have an intensely flavored treat.*

7 tablespoons unsalted butter

6 large peaches, peeled & sliced

½ pint blackberries

⅓ cup sugar

¾ teaspoon cinnamon

½ teaspoon mace

Juice of ½ lemon

8 sheets filo dough,
   at room temperature

Confectioners' sugar

Preheat the oven to 400°F. Using 1 tablespoon of the butter, generously grease a 12¼-inch cazuela.

In a small saucepan, melt 4 tablespoons of the butter. Set aside.

In a large nonreactive bowl, toss the peaches and blackberries with the sugar, cinnamon, mace, and lemon juice. Arrange the fruit mixture over the bottom of the cazuela. Cut the remaining butter into thin chips and dot over the fruit.

Lay the filo out flat on a countertop and cover with a damp kitchen towel. Transfer 1 sheet of the filo to a work surface and brush it generously with the melted butter. Gently pick up the buttered dough and loosely crumple it into a ball about 4 inches in diameter. Place the crumpled filo on top of the fruit in the cazuela. Repeat with the remaining filo, leaving some space between crumples for the juices to bubble up as the fruit cooks.

Bake for 10 minutes. Reduce the oven temperature to 325°F and bake for 20 minutes longer, or until the edges of the filo are light brown. Sprinkle generously

with confectioners' sugar. Raise the oven temperature to 400°F and bake for 8 to 10 minutes, or until the sugar melts to a glaze.

Let the crumple stand for up to 1 hour. Serve while still warm; the filo will get soggy if the crumple stands for too long. **Serves 6 to 8.**

Banana Bread Pudding

*Using a heavy earthenware casserole and a low oven temperature
enables you to bake this decadent pudding without using a
hot water bath. The result is golden-topped, creamy-textured bread
surrounded by lush, flan-like custard.*

5 tablespoons unsalted butter
½ cup golden raisins
1 baguette
4 large eggs
2 large egg yolks
⅔ cup sugar

1 cup pureed very ripe banana
   (about 2 medium bananas)
3 cups milk
½ cup heavy cream
2 tablespoons rum or brandy
1 teaspoon pure vanilla extract

Preheat the oven to 275°F. Using 1 tablespoon of the butter, generously grease a 12¼-inch cazuela. Sprinkle the raisins over the bottom of the dish and set aside.

Cut 16 (1¼-inch) slices from the bread. With the remaining butter, butter the slices of bread. Arrange the slices, buttered side up, in one layer in the cazuela.

In a medium-size bowl, whisk the eggs and egg yolks together. Add the sugar and whisk to combine. Mix in the bananas, milk, cream, liquor, and vanilla, until well combined. Pour the mixture over the sliced bread. Let sit for 15 minutes so the bread soaks up some of the liquid.

Bake for 1 hour, until the custard has pulled away from the sides of the cazuela and the tops of the bread slices are lightly browned; the custard will still be slightly soft in the center. Let sit for 15 to 20 minutes before serving. **Serves 8 to 10.**

WEIGHTS

OUNCES AND POUNDS	METRICS
¼ ounce~~~~~~~~~~~~~~~~~	7 grams
⅓ ounce ~~~~~~~~~~~~~~~	10 grams
½ ounce ~~~~~~~~~~~~~~~	14 grams
1 ounce ~~~~~~~~~~~~~~~	28 grams
1½ ounces ~~~~~~~~~~~~~	42 grams
1¾ ounces~~~~~~~~~~~~~~	50 grams
2 ounces~~~~~~~~~~~~~~~	57 grams
3 ounces~~~~~~~~~~~~~~~	85 grams
3½ ounces~~~~~~~~~~~~~~	100 grams
4 ounces (¼ pound) ~~~~~~~	114 grams
6 ounces~~~~~~~~~~~~~~~	170 grams
8 ounces (½ pound) ~~~~~~~	227 grams
9 ounces~~~~~~~~~~~~~~~	250 grams
16 ounces (1 pound)~~~~~~~	464 grams

LIQUID MEASURES

tsp.: teaspoon
Tbs.: tablespoon

SPOONS AND CUPS	METRIC EQUIVALENTS
¼ tsp.~~~~~~~~~~~~~~	1.23 milliliters
½ tsp.~~~~~~~~~~~~~~	2.5 milliliters
¾ tsp.~~~~~~~~~~~~~~	3.7 milliliters
1 tsp.~~~~~~~~~~~~~~	5 milliliters
1 dessertspoon ~~~~~~~~	10 milliliters
1 Tbs. (3 tsp.) ~~~~~~~~	15 milliliters
2 Tbs. (1 ounce) ~~~~~~~	30 milliliters
¼ cup ~~~~~~~~~~~~~	60 milliliters
⅓ cup ~~~~~~~~~~~~~	80 milliliters
½ cup ~~~~~~~~~~~~~	120 milliliters
⅔ cup ~~~~~~~~~~~~~	160 milliliters
¾ cup ~~~~~~~~~~~~~	180 milliliters
1 cup (8 ounces) ~~~~~~~	240 milliliters
2 cups (1 pint) ~~~~~~~~	480 milliliters
3 cups~~~~~~~~~~~~~~	720 milliliters
4 cups (1 quart)~~~~~~~~	1 liter
4 quarts (1 gallon) ~~~~~~	3¾ liters

TEMPERATURES

°F (FAHRENHEIT)	°C (CENTIGRADE OR CELSIUS)
32 (water freezes) ~~~~~~~~~~~	0
200 ~~~~~~~~~~~~~~~~~~~~	95
212 (water boils)~~~~~~~~~~~~	100
250 ~~~~~~~~~~~~~~~~~~~~	120
275 ~~~~~~~~~~~~~~~~~~~~	135
300 (slow oven)~~~~~~~~~~~~~	150
325 ~~~~~~~~~~~~~~~~~~~~	160
350 (moderate oven)~~~~~~~~~~	175
375 ~~~~~~~~~~~~~~~~~~~~	190
400 (hot oven) ~~~~~~~~~~~~~	205
425 ~~~~~~~~~~~~~~~~~~~~	220
450 (very hot oven) ~~~~~~~~~	232
475 ~~~~~~~~~~~~~~~~~~~~	245
500 (extremely hot oven)~~~~~~	260

LENGTH

U.S. MEASUREMENTS	METRIC EQUIVALENTS
⅛ inch~~~~~~~~~~~~~~~~	3mm
¼ inch~~~~~~~~~~~~~~~~	6mm
⅜ inch~~~~~~~~~~~~~~~~	1 cm
½ inch~~~~~~~~~~~~~~~~	1.2 cm
¾ inch~~~~~~~~~~~~~~~~	2 cm
1 inch ~~~~~~~~~~~~~~~~	2.5 cm
1¼ inches~~~~~~~~~~~~~~	3.1 cm
1½ inches~~~~~~~~~~~~~~	3.7 cm
2 inches ~~~~~~~~~~~~~~	5 cm
3 inches ~~~~~~~~~~~~~~	7.5 cm
4 inches ~~~~~~~~~~~~~~	10 cm
5 inches ~~~~~~~~~~~~~~	12.5 cm

APPROXIMATE EQUIVALENTS

1 kilo is slightly more than 2 pounds
1 liter is slightly more than 1 quart
1 meter is slightly over 3 feet
1 centimeter is approximately ⅜ inch

INDEX